REAL ENGAGEMENT

How do I help my students become motivated, confident, and self-directed learners?

Allison **ZMUDA** | Robyn R. **JACKSON**

ASCD   Alexandria, VA USA

ASCD | arias™

Website: www.ascd.org www.ascdarias.org
E-mail: books@ascd.org

Copyright © 2015 by Allison Zmuda & Robyn R. Jackson. All rights reserved. It is illegal to reproduce copies of this work in print or electronic format (including reproductions displayed on a secure intranet or stored in a retrieval system or other electronic storage device from which copies can be made or displayed) without the prior written permission of the publisher. Readers who wish to duplicate this copyrighted material may do so for a small fee by contacting the Copyright Clearance Center (CCC), 222 Rosewood Dr., Danvers, MA 01923, USA (phone: 978-750-8400; fax: 978-646-8600; web: www.copyright.com). To inquire about site licensing options or any other reuse, contact ASCD Permissions at www.ascd.org/permissions, permissions@ascd.org, or 703-575-5749. Send translation inquiries to translations@ascd.org.

Printed in the United States of America. Cover art © 2015 by ASCD.

ASCD publications present a variety of viewpoints. The views expressed or implied in this book should not be interpreted as official positions of the Association.

ASCD LEARN TEACH LEAD® and ASCD ARIAS™ are trademarks owned by ASCD and may not be used without permission. All other referenced trademarks are the property of their respective owners.

PAPERBACK ISBN: 978-1-4166-2070-9   ASCD product # SF115056
Also available as an e-book (see Books in Print for the ISBNs).

Library of Congress Cataloging-in-Publication Data
Zmuda, Allison.
  Real engagement : how do I help my students become motivated, confident, and self-directed learners? / Allison Zmuda Robyn R. Jackson.
    pages cm
  Includes bibliographical references and index.
  ISBN 978-1-4166-2070-9 (pbk. : alk. paper) 1. Motivation in education. 2. Engagement (Philosophy) 3. Effective teaching. 4. Learning, Psychology of. 5. Self-culture. 6. Study skills. I. Title.
  LB1065.Z58 2015
  370.15'4--dc23

                    2015009464

24 23 22 21 20 19 18 17 16 15   1 2 3 4 5 6 7 8 9 10

REAL ENGAGEMENT

How do I help my students become motivated, confident, and self-directed learners?

Want to earn a free ASCD Arias e-book?
Your opinion counts! Please take 2–3 minutes to give
us your feedback on this publication. All survey
respondents will be entered into a drawing to
win an ASCD Arias e-book.

Please visit
www.ascd.org/ariasfeedback

Thank you!

Real Engagement
(Instead of Compliance)

No teacher wants a classroom full of bored and lethargic students who put their heads on their desks the moment the lesson starts, shrug and stare blankly when called on, and blithely scribble the convenient answer when completing their work—assuming that they complete their work at all. If you're like us or the teachers we serve in our workshops, you came to teaching for something more. You came to teaching to inspire your students to learn, and to create a classroom space where you and your students work together to achieve insight and understanding.

So when it comes to student engagement, you're active and committed. You keep an eye out for new strategies and the latest tricks that will help you gain and maintain your students' attention. You look to jazz up your lessons, seek hooks that will startle and delight your students, and find new ways of presenting the material that will get them excited about the task ahead. And, if you're honest, sometimes it feels like you're killing yourself to line up this dog and pony show each day.

You're not alone. We see this all the time—dedicated teachers who are working incredibly hard to be "inspiring" and chasing just the right combination of lesson elements that will get their students interested, involved, and actively learning. What they generally wind up with, aside from a case of acute exhaustion, are classrooms composed of compliant, dutiful learners who willingly follow directions, complete assignments, meet requirements, and stay on task. But the real engagement these teachers are pursuing—with students asking intriguing questions, enthusiastically immersing themselves in projects and assignments, seeking feedback on their performance, and taking pride in their progress—remains elusive.

If you're reading this book, chances are you've asked this question: "Why is it so hard to get all of my students to be fully engaged and deeply involved in their own learning?" The answer may surprise you. You see, it's not that you aren't trying hard enough; it's that you are probably using the wrong set of strategies. Real engagement doesn't come from tricks and gimmicks; it's something you enable, not something you achieve. It happens when you use a few simple keys to help your students own, manage, and pursue their own learning.

What's So Bad About Compliance?

"OK, take out your math textbooks and turn to page 72," Mrs. Levenson says as she walks briskly to the front of the room and begins writing a sentence on the board.

The students pull their math texts from their desks or backpacks, turn to the designated page, and wait quietly for her next instructions.

"Today, we are going to learn the order of operations," Mrs. Levenson begins. Pointing the sentence she's written, she continues, "I want you to repeat after me. *Please excuse my dear Aunt Sally.*"

"Please excuse my dear Aunt Sally," the students repeat.

"Again, please," Mrs. Levenson instructs, pointing.

"Please excuse my dear Aunt Sally."

"Very good," she smiles at the class. "Now, this sentence is actually an acrostic. Who here remembers what an acrostic is?"

A few hands begin to go up. Mrs. Levenson waits until she sees at least five, then calls on Jeremy.

"It's a sentence where the first letter of each word really stands for something else," Jeremy explains.

Mrs. Levenson nods. "Thank you, Jeremy," she says. "Next time, I'd like to see more hands up. Now, eyes on me, please." She pauses a moment until all students are facing her. "The *P* stands for *parentheses*," she continues, writing the word on the board. "What does the *P* stand for?" she prompts the class.

"Parentheses," they repeat in unison.

"Good. The *E* stands for *exponents*." She writes *exponents* on the board. "What does the *E* stand for?"

"Exponents," the students repeat.

"I didn't hear everyone," Mrs. Levenson says. "Taylor, eyes on me. I don't want anyone to lose participation points today." She waits quietly while Taylor turns and faces her. "Thank you. Now, Taylor, what does the *E* stand for?"

"Exponents," Taylor reads from the board.

"Yes." Mrs. Levenson turns back to the board. "Moving on," she continues, "the *M* stands for *multiply*, and the *D* stands for *divide,*" She writes *multiply* and, below it, *divide.* "OK, class, what do we have so far, then?" She points to each of the words, and students recite them aloud.

"Good," Mrs. Levenson says. So, class, if the *M* stands for *multiply,* and the *D* stands for *divide,* what do you think the *A* stands for?"

She surveys the room as a few students raise their hands. "Remember," she says, "the way you show me that you know the answer is to raise your hand."

More hands go up.

Mrs. Levenson smiles. "Good. I see almost all of you have your hand raised." She points to Antonio.

"*Add*?" he offers.

"I need your answer in a complete sentence, Antonio," Mrs. Levenson prompts.

Antonio tries again. "The *A* stands for *add*?"

"Yes. Very good, Anthony." Mrs. Levenson adds *add* to the growing list. From the corner of her eye, she sees Amber's hand still up. "Amber, honey, you can put your hand down now."

"But I have a question," Amber says.

Mrs. Levenson turns to Amber. "What's your question?"

"We learned to add first, before we learned to multiply, so why does *add* come after *multiply*?"

"That's a great question, Amber," Mrs. Levenson smiles, glancing up at the clock. "But let's wait until we get through this part of the lesson, and then we'll get back to it."

Amber puts her hand down slowly, and Mrs. Levenson turns back to the board. "OK, where were we? Ah yes, we know what the *P* stands for, and we know what the *E* stands for. We know that *M* stands for *multiply* and *D* stands for *divide*. And Antonio just told us that *A* stands for *add*. So, who can tell me what the *S* stands for?"

Several students raise their hands.

"I see that Kaitlin knows, and Ramon knows, and Asia knows," Mrs. Levenson notes. "Haile knows, and Ryan knows, and Selene knows, and JaBare knows. Good." She points to Miri, who hasn't raised her hand. "Miri, do you know what the *S* stands for?"

"The *S* stands for *subtract*," Miri replies quietly.

"Miri, I want to hear you say that with conviction," Mrs. Levenson prompts.

"The *S* stands for *subtract*," Miri says more loudly.

"Good, Miri," Mrs. Levenson smiles, writing *subtract*. "We're ready now to go over the entire thing." She points to the list of words she has recorded on the board. "All together now, please."

"Parentheses, exponents, multiply, divide, add, subtract."

"With conviction!" urges Mrs. Levenson.

"Parentheses, exponents, multiply, divide, add, subtract!"

Smiling broadly, Mrs. Levenson turns to her students. "Good! Now you know the order of operations."

Mrs. Levenson has classroom full of compliant students. She works hard for that compliance, and given the choice between what we see here and outwardly defiant, disrespectful, defensive, or totally checked-out students, it doesn't seem so bad. At least everyone is quiet and participating in the work. At least the lesson is moving forward. But teachers who settle for compliance are shortchanging their students and themselves.

Compliant students may be tuned in to you, to the lesson, and to the textbook, but they are not fully tuned in to learning. They may be focused on getting the right answer, gaining your approval, or earning a good grade, but they aren't pushing themselves to dig deeper or to get something meaningful and personal from the learning experience.

In a nutshell, the problem with compliance is that it is just another form of disengagement—of students not being invested in their own learning. Because they don't feel an innate connection to the content, they are always teetering on the edge of being bored and tuning out, and they rely heavily on you (and the hooks, tricks, and "fun" assignments you might employ) to make what they are learning seem relevant and appealing. That's a lot of pressure for you to bear.

There's another kind of pressure that comes with compliance. It's the sneaky little voice in your head whispering that you and your students could be doing so much more. Are you all just going through the motions of learning? Are any of you really doing the important work you've come to the classroom to do?

What Is Real Engagement?

"OK, take out your math textbooks and turn to page 72," Mrs. Elliott announces, walking briskly to the front of the room and writing a sentence on the board. "Veronica," she adds, "it's time to put away your journal."

"I'm almost finished," Veronica says, continuing to write.

"Wow, you must be on a roll," Mrs. Elliott smiles. "Finish the entry you're working on, and then put your journal away, take out your math textbook, and join us."

Veronica nods and continues to write.

Meanwhile, Mrs. Elliott turns to the rest of the class. "Today, we are going to learn about the order of operations. It's a tool we can use to figure out problems like the ones on page 72. Take a look at problem #1, and tell me what you notice about it."

The students look at their textbooks, with some leaning over to make a comment to a neighbor, and some picking up pencils and beginning to copy the problem. Mrs. Elliott waits for few seconds and then calls everyone back to order. "OK, tell me. What do you notice?"

Several hands go up. Mrs. Elliott calls on Matthew.

"What I notice is that all these problems look really hard," Matthew says, shaking his head.

"OK, Matthew, what about the problems looks hard?" Mrs. Elliott prompts.

Charlotte interrupts, "They have a lot of symbols!"

Mrs. Elliott frowns slightly. "Charlotte, honey, remember to raise your hand." She turns back to Matthew. "Matthew, what about these problems looks hard?"

Matthew studies the page for a few seconds. "I mean, I see what Charlotte said about all the symbols, but I am trying to do the math in my head, and I keep getting stuck."

"Why do you think you keep getting stuck, Matthew?" Mrs. Elliott asks.

"Mrs. Elliott, what does this symbol here mean?" James asks, holding up his textbook and pointing to an exponent.

"Hand up, James. That's called an exponent. Remember, we learned about those two weeks ago."

"We did?" James asks. "Oh, yeah. They're things like squared or to the fourth power?"

"Exactly," Mrs. Elliott nods. "Matthew, do you want some time to think about this more?"

Matthew nods as he scribbles a problem onto a sheet of paper.

"What's that sentence on the board?" Shelly asks.

"That sentence is a memory device that can help us learn and remember the order of operations. Once you learn the order of operations, problems like these won't seem so hard. Yes? You have a question, Melanie?"

"You have an aunt named Sally?"

"No, I don't actually have an Aunt Sally," Mrs. Elliott smiles. "That's just there to help us remember." She walks back to the board and underlines the first letter in each word. "Each of these letters stands for something else. For instance, this *P* stands for *parentheses*." Mrs. Elliott writes the word *parentheses* on the board.

"Why is *parentheses* first?" Charlotte asks. "Oh, I forgot!" she adds, putting her hand in the air.

Mrs. Elliott smiles and writes a math problem on the board. "Thank you for raising your hand, Charlotte. And that's a good question. Let's take a look at problem #1 and focus on this part inside the parentheses. Parentheses tell us that all the numbers they contain have to stay together. And, by simplifying the part of the problem *inside* the parentheses in some way, we can make solving the entire problem a whole lot easier. Matthew, you are working on problem #1 right now. Have you tried solving the part in the parentheses first?"

"No, no! Don't TELL me!" Matthew replies, covering his ears and bending even closer to his paper.

"Sorry, Matthew, I was just trying to help," Mrs. Elliott apologizes. Turning back to the class, she continues, "In a complicated problem, solve within the parentheses first. Does that make sense?"

A few students nod.

"Charlotte, does that make sense to you?"

"I think so," Charlotte says, staring at the problem. "What about all the other stuff?"

Mrs. Elliott turns back to the board and points to the underlined *E*. "Once we deal with what's inside the parentheses, the next step is to deal with the exponents," she explains, writing the word. "And what are exponents, James?"

"Those little numbers that tell you to square something or make something to the third power or whatever," he replies.

"They tell you how many times you have to multiply a number by itself," clarifies Kerry.

"Right," Mrs. Elliott agrees. "Hey, Veronica?" she says. "Last sentence, please."

"I know! I'm almost done," Veronica says.

"OK, so we know that the *P* stands for *parentheses*, and the *E* stands for *exponents*," Mrs. Elliott says, pointing to the words on the board. "The *M* stands for . . . ?"

"*Murder,*" Jackson says, sinisterly.

The class laughs.

"Nice try, Jackson," Mrs. Elliott smiles. "The *M* stands for a math word. Take a look at problem #1, and see if you can figure out *which* math word. Don't worry about raising your hand here. Just call it out."

"*Math!*" Justin blurts.

"*Method?*" guesses Ariana.

"Look at the problem we're trying to solve," Mrs. Elliott prompts again. "Imagine we've already taken care of the work within the parentheses and the exponents. What other symbols are left?"

The students stare at the problem for a moment.

"*Multiply!*" Peter exclaims. "There's a multiplication symbol."

"You guys, stop it!" Matthew protests. "I almost have it."

"Sorry, Matthew," Mrs. Elliott apologizes, walking to his desk. "I know you want to do this yourself." She looks over his shoulder at his work. "Hmmm, you do almost have it. I tell you what. Why don't you go out into the hall and finish that problem? That way, we won't disturb you. Come back in once you've figured it out so that you can explain your method to us, or come back in if you want help."

"I won't need help!" Matthew grabs his papers and heads to the door.

Mrs. Elliott turns back to the class. "OK, we've got *P* for *parentheses*, *E* for *exponents*, and *M* for *multiply*. So what do you think the *D*, the *A*, and the *S* stand for? Somebody shout them out."

"*Divide!*" Charlotte shouts, smiling at Mrs. Elliott.

"Yes!" Mrs. Elliott shouts at the same pitch. As everyone laughs, she continues, "Yes, the *D* stands for *divide*. How did you figure that out, Charlotte?"

Charlotte shrugs. "It just made sense," she says. "If you are gonna multiply, then you will have to divide. There isn't any division in that first problem, but there's division in a bunch of the others."

Mrs. Elliott pats Charlotte on shoulder as she makes her way to Veronica's desk. "Veronica, time's up."

"But I'm almost finished! Just give me a minute more. . . ."

"I know it's important, but we are doing important work here, too. Put your journal away."

Veronica scribbles a few more words then reluctantly closes her journal.

"Thank you, Veronica," Mrs. Elliott says, smiling. "I know you were really engrossed in your work. If you want, you can stay in during recess and finish. For now, take out your math book and turn to page 72."

Veronica nods and fishes the textbook from her desk. Charlotte leans over and points to the problem that the class is working on.

"We only have two operations left, signified by *A* and *S*," Mrs. Elliott continues. "Turn to a partner, and tell your partner what you think the *A* and the *S* stand for."

The students turn and talk. After 30 seconds, Mrs. Elliott calls the question. "Class, what do we think the *A* and the *S* stand for?"

"*Add* and *subtract*," they call in unison.

"That's right!" Mrs. Elliott smiles, as she writes the two words on the board. "Good job. Let's say the whole thing together."

"Parentheses, exponents, multiply, divide, add, and subtract."

"Good," Mrs. Elliott smiles. "*That* is the order of operations. Now let's take a look at problem #2 and use the order of operations to figure out how we're going to go about solving it. We aren't going to try to solve the problem yet; I just want you to tell me where we would start, what we would do next, and so on."

"Wait, what about that sentence?" Chase calls out.

"What sentence?" asks Mrs. Elliott.

"That one." Chase points and reads, "*Please excuse my dear Aunt Sally.*"

"Oh, that. Remember, that is just a way to help you remember the order of operations."

"Hey, Mrs. Elliott, can I make it *Please excuse my dear Aunt Shelly*?" Shelly asks.

"That's fine, Shelly."

"I wanna make it *Put every dog at soccer,*" Michael offers.

"That doesn't make any sense!" Shelly insists. "It has to make sense."

"It's your memory tool, so you can make it whatever you want," Mrs. Elliott intervenes. "Choose whatever will help you to remember the order of operations so that you can use it in your work."

Real engagement is when students choose to invest (and reinvest) their attention and effort in the pursuit of a learning goal. As the example of Mrs. Elliott's classroom shows us, truly engaged students don't want to be "spoon fed" content. They want to think on their own and figure things out for themselves. They are willing to struggle, to grapple with new concepts, and to reach for new understanding even when doing so is difficult.

Another sign of real engagement is that students take care and pride in the work they produce. They revise not because it's a requirement or a way to gain 10 extra points, but because they want to. They evaluate their work and tinker with it until it meets not only their teacher's standards but their standards as well. That's because truly engaged students aren't "just in it for the grade," nor are they marking time and "just trying to get through the class." They come to the classroom with their own objectives, and they evaluate their learning and their learning experience in light of these very personal goals. They are not satisfied if they make a great grade but fail to achieve what they'd set out to do.

Because their learning goals are personal, truly engaged students will seek out ways to make the work relevant. Assignments and projects have to mean something. If their teacher doesn't provide that relevance, they will seek it out on their own, even if that means going beyond the assignment's original parameters. They are willing to go a step further, to take a different route, to propose an alternative in pursuit of their own ideas. They are curious and inclined to pursue tangents that seem interesting. And they are willing to try something new, even if it's uncomfortable, if they believe doing so will take them closer to their learning goals.

Why Real Engagement Matters

Real engagement matters because it invites students to not only participate in the learning process but ultimately take ownership of their own learning in a way that goes far beyond the walls of the classroom. So while real engagement does prepare students for the increasingly rigorous external assessments they must face, it also prepares them for the real-life measures awaiting them on the job and in their personal lives.

The overview of compliant and engaged students in Figure 1 paints a picture of what behaviors you might see in your students. As you read what the engaged learner does, you will pick up an undercurrent of impulsiveness, defiance, and insistence that can be construed as "disrespectful." Real engagement, as much as we advocate it, isn't a golden ticket to the classroom of your dreams; it's more like a passport to the next level of instruction, where the challenges are different and the stakes are higher, but the rewards are much greater.

Now that you understand what real engagement is, the next question is how to bring it to your classroom. There are four keys to real engagement: **clarity**, **context**, **challenge**, and **culture**. We have paired each of the four keys with a reflective question—an anchor that will help you think

FIGURE 1: **A Compliant Learner and an Engaged One**

Compliant, Dutiful Learner	Engaged Learner
Follows oral and written directions with minimal prompting	Follows oral and written directions with minimal prompting but may pursue an alternative approach to personalize the experience
Completes explicit procedures and requirements in a timely manner	Pursues own train of thought regardless of task at hand or feedback from staff, which may make it difficult to finish in a timely manner
Intently focuses on task completion to finish the assignment	Focuses on the learning and wants to talk about it regardless of prompting and without consideration of others
Participates in group activities and discussion when prompted	Actively participates in group activities and discussion when interested in the material but can be reticent while still mulling over ideas and information or when still actively immersed in the previous task
Responds to straightforward questions but needs scaffolding to pursue a more complex question	May be bored or unmotivated to respond to straightforward questions but is fascinated by questions that require teasing out ambiguity and complexity or questions that are personally interesting and relevant

FIGURE 1: **A Compliant Learner and an Engaged One** (*continued*)

Compliant, Dutiful Learner	Engaged Learner
Seeks approval, credit, or high marks because of effort, quantity, or adherence to directions	Seeks recognition for the thoughtfulness of the work or originality of the work, even if it isn't complete or doesn't adhere to the directions
Plays it safe by electing to follow known procedures, explore familiar topics, and use tools that have been mastered; dismisses or avoids alternative points of view or approaches	Chooses to take risks by exploring something new, attempts to solve a problem in a novel way, and considers alternative points of view
Completes work with no expectation for finding personal relevance, connection, or interest	Seeks work that is interesting—or seeks to make work interesting
Takes information at face value and does not question the credibility or validity of "experts" (e.g., a teacher, an online source, the textbook's interpretation)	Questions both text and people to better understand an issue, topic, or problem
Waits patiently for assistance to get help or decides not to ask a question because the conversation would require more work	Demands immediate assistance or attention and feels justified for doing so in light of curiosity, interest, or investment in the task or topic

through and design learning experiences, adjust assignments, and build a classroom environment that will more
deeply engage students in their own learning:

- **Clarity**—"What am I asking students to do?"
- **Context**—"Why is it important?"
- **Challenge**—"How does it stretch my students?"
- **Culture**—"How do I show my support?"

In the remainder of this book, we'll take a closer look
at these keys and questions and explore why they matter to
students. We will also offer specific strategies for providing
clarity, providing context, providing challenge, and building a
supportive classroom culture that will help you help your students become motivated, confident, and self-directed learners.

Clarity

The question associated with **clarity** is **"What am I asking
students to do?"**

To answer this question, you must identify and articulate
the learning targets—or goals—in a way that really focuses
your teaching. Research has demonstrated that goal clarity
supports engagement in two ways: it ensures that you design
assignments that are worth doing, and it provides parameters for how you will work with students to further their
development as independent learners (Wiggins & McTighe,
2005, 2011).

When we talk about learning targets, we mean both the large, long-term goals that are appropriate for a course or a program and the smaller, short-term goals set for lessons and units. Let's look an example from elementary geometry. If the long-term K–5 geometry goal is *by the end of grade 5, students should be able to independently identify, describe, compare, classify, and analyze geometric figures to explain the world around them,* a 2nd grade teacher might identify two short-term goals that will help students get there and translate both into student-friendly language: (1) *I can describe and compare plane and solid figures,* and (2) *I can identify and create figures with at least one line of symmetry.*

With these short- and long-term goals in mind, the teacher would then take a look at each of her assignments to determine whether it is "in" or "out" and make modifications, as needed. She would pay special attention to the second verb in each of the short-term goal statements—*compare* and *create*—as those expectations require meaning making and application. *Compare* asks students to look at plane and solid figures to identify common attributes. Because the long-term goal focuses students on being able to use geometric figures to explain the world around them, the teacher might have students go on an expedition to find examples of spheres, cubes, and rectangular prisms. *Create* requires students to make something for a given purpose, so she might have students to play with manipulatives (e.g., pipe cleaners, geometric solids, or geoboards) and then have them design a figure where symmetry is important (e.g., a flag or a human face). Adjusting lessons to incorporate short-term goals that have a clear connection to long-term goals gives teaching focus and context. And it helps students engage more meaningfully in their work because they know that the work they are doing is getting them closer to those larger goals.

Goal clarity also fosters student independence. Every teacher has experienced the temptation to be "too helpful" to students: to provide too many scaffolds, offer too many directions, and ask too many small questions. These efforts are well intentioned, but they wind up "saving" students from doing the intensive thinking and transfer that deep learning requires. We will talk more about "not saving students" in the sections devoted to **challenge** and **culture**, but it's worth making the point here that your goal as a teacher should be to build your students' autonomy so that they can handle both the straightforward assignments and the messy ones.

Why Clarity Matters to Students

Whenever students encounter an assignment or activity in class, they ask themselves two questions: (1) "What, exactly, am I supposed to do?" and (2) "What's the point of doing it?"

Unless you give students good answers to these questions, they will either be confused or go through the motions of the assignment with little commitment. Goal clarity on a given assignment serves as a "North Star" that helps students focus on the work's purpose and prevents them from getting tangled in a web of problems, questions, or prompts. If the ultimate aim of schooling is student independence, then creating goal clarity helps students successfully move back and forth between the big picture and the details of a specific assignment.

What You Can Do to Provide Clarity

Identify the overarching goals for the course or program. Think about your long-term goals—what it is that you are training students to do in a given subject by the end of the grade level, the completion of the course, or the end of the level of schooling (i.e., elementary, middle, or high school). The most powerful way to articulate these long-term goals is to work in vertical teams (building or district) to determine the common threads in the state, ministry, or national frameworks and then put these into language that is accessible and purposeful for teacher and student alike. For example, a vertical K–12 science team might examine the Next Generation Science Standards to make sense of how engineering is woven throughout a student's K–12 experience. Engineering is a new area of focus for most science teachers, and it starts in kindergarten with the expectation that students be able to develop a simple model to represent an amount, relationship, relative scale, or pattern. The team could take that understanding and use it as the basis for the following long-term goal statement for kindergartners: *I can design (and redesign) a model by creating a solution, testing it out, and evaluating how to make it better.*

Identifying long-term goals as a group of colleagues is a powerful practice. It allows teachers to make sense of what the standards really mean, talk through examples or ideas for assignments, and collectively agree on each long-term goal as a big deal that is worth spending time on within and across grade levels. Articulating these goals provides students with a context and reason for doing the work, and it gives them parameters for doing the work meaningfully and well.

Identify the short-term learning targets for a given unit. Break your long-term goals into goals that are smaller, more concrete, and more specific. Make these the explicit targets of multiple learning opportunities, and give students plenty of time to practice the associated skills, self-evaluate, and improve. Keep in mind that a good learning target is stated in a way that clarifies for students the reason behind the assignment. For example, a short-term learning target in physics class might be *I can explain how motion deals with the changes of an object's position over time.* The students might work to achieve that target through a range of text readings, problems, and challenges. An example from 3rd grade reading might be *I can find the main idea and show how details support it.* The students could read a variety of nonfiction newspaper articles covering both areas that they are interested in and areas where they have little to no knowledge.

Design assignments that align with the long-term goals and short-term learning targets. Before you get too far down the road with developing a new assignment, make sure it actually is designed to measure students' mastery of the meaningful goal you have agreed on. For example, a library media specialist and a social studies teacher might set out to teach their students to *create research questions; seek,* *evaluate, and make sense of new information; and present research findings.* But if the research assignment students actually get is a fact-gathering mission that culminates in writing a multiparagraph summary of key aspects of a particular topic, the specialist and teacher are not moving the students toward the stated, important goal. A better choice for working toward this long-term goal would be an authentic assignment designed to highlight the value of research, which could be tailored to various topics and grade levels. For example:

- *An annotated bibliography:* Research a given topic and produce a thesis statement as well as a list of the most promising sources that includes a brief summary of each and how it may be valuable in relation to the thesis statement.
- *A debate or an expert panel:* Communicate deep knowledge on a given topic (or point of view) based on research, evidence, and relevant experience, for a given purpose and target audience.
- *A position statement:* Develop an argument through location, evaluation, and analysis of primary and secondary sources using supporting information and persuasive rhetoric for a given purpose and target audience.
- *A critique or review:* Using an established set of criteria, evaluate a text, performance, or organization, and use relevant evidence to support that evaluation for a given purpose and target audience.

Notice how the foundation for each of these assignments is a meaningful experience that builds students' concrete research skills and aligns closely with the course's larger goal. When you are designing assignments, continually ask yourself two questions: (1) "What is it that I am trying to do for my students?" and (2) "Does this assignment lead my students to that destination?"

Eliminate the guesswork about what it is you really want. Assignment directions that are muddled or confusing force students to figure out what the assignment is before they can engage with the assignment itself. On the other hand, assignment directions that are overly prescriptive and demand that students obey the step-by-step instructions can lead to a predictable and uninspired result. Go through your assignment directions and revise them to clarify what the assignment requires (the non-negotiables) and where students can customize the work to cater to their strengths, incorporate their areas of interest, and give fuller play to their original ideas. To support the parameters of the assignment, provide a rubric that indicates what quality looks like, written in student-friendly language.

Make sure that students can articulate what they are doing and why they are doing it. A simple strategy to help students engage in learning from the start is to provide a written statement of the learning target and ask them to rephrase it in their own words. Another strategy is to ask students to point to evidence of that learning target, either in their own work or another's work. You might also encourage visitors to your classroom to engage students in discussion of their assignment and its purpose.

Context

The question associated with **context** is **"Why is this work important?"**

Goal clarity and the establishment of context go hand in hand. Clarity articulates what students must do, and context provides students with a frame of reference and helps them grasp why the work matters. When you ask why an assignment or project is important, your answer will fall into one of two categories:

1. *It has external significance*—meaning that the topic, subject, or outcome of the work is significant to a given community or has an impact on others in the world.

2. *It has internal significance*—meaning that the topic, subject, or outcome of the work has personal significance to students, addressing a challenge, inquiry, or idea that connects with their own family, culture, interests, aspirations, and views.

Assignments that have *external significance* typically are problem- or performance-based. They often feature a challenge to be met that students recognize as worth the time, attention, and revision required to get it right, especially when the audience for the work extends beyond the teacher. Research confirms that when students are invested in authentic problems, challenges, or inquiries, they are more likely to sustain attention over time, become more knowledgeable about the subject, and improve upon a range of skills (Barron & Darling-Hammond, 2007; Holm, 2011).

Here are some examples of assignments with external significance, drawn from secondary school disciplines:

- *Mathematics:* Calculating "the true cost" of major events (e.g., natural disaster, going to college, owning a car).
- *Science:* Figuring out how to clean up a man-made mess (e.g., oil spill, carbon in the atmosphere, water pollution).
- *Civics/government:* Looking at the challenges of low voter turnout and determining what policies or practices would get citizens to the polls.
- *Career and technical education:* Collaborating to construct a boat that is "seaworthy" and then testing it out in a local body of water.

Assignments that have *internal significance* typically involve work that connects authentically to who students are and how they see the world. Once again, some secondary school examples:

- *English/language arts:* Exploring the theme of justice through multiple assigned texts (e.g., *Ninth Ward, Holes, To Kill a Mockingbird, The Republic, The Merchant of Venice*) as well as student-discovered artifacts (e.g., historical and contemporary photographs, memorable lyrics) and the student's original works of self-expression (e.g., personal narratives, poems, drawings).

- *World languages:* Assembling a list of personally meaningful objects from childhood (e.g., a stuffed bear, a first bicycle), generating descriptions, and explaining these objects' significance.
- *Advisory program:* Articulating an aspiration (e.g., "Here's what I want to do to add value to the world . . .") and then taking action toward it by engaging in research; participating in an internship; or working on a proposal, project, or performance.

Why Context Matters to Students

Students want to do work that matters rather than feel like they are trapped in a bureaucracy, just performing their assigned role until the bell rings. A bureaucratic learning experience is tedious, wearisome, and predictable; if students are on board, they're essentially just along for the ride. An engaging learning experience is demanding, inspiring, and sometimes exasperating; each student is in the driver's seat, directing his or her own execution of an idea or pursuit of an answer or understanding.

In performance-based disciplines like drama, music, and technical education, drill and application are inseparable. Assignments like rehearsing a monologue, practicing chords, or fixing a piece of equipment by following the instructions in a technical manual are both preparation for performance and performance itself. It's pretty clear, for example, that you have to practice chords in order to play chords. In other disciplines, the connections between drill and application are less clear. There, a teacher's work to build necessary foundational knowledge can sometimes crowd out opportunities for meaningful application. Students in a science class may not be asked to independently design and carry out a full investigation. Students in a math class may not be given tricky problems that require background research. Students in a U.S. history class may never get to analyze contemporary problems by tracing these problems back to their historical roots. Students in an English class may not be asked to create a repository of ideas, phrases, and questions for the purpose of exploring these in their own writing. Without assignments that offer application opportunities for the skills and understanding students are being asked to develop, they are left to wonder, "Why is this work important?" and "Why is this work important to *me*?" If they do not get good answers to these questions, the compliant ones may complete the assignments, but they will not personally invest in them. If you want real engagement from students, you must help them understand the context of every learning experience.

What You Can Do to Provide Context

Identify the "why" for yourself. It is important that you understand and can articulate why you are teaching what you are teaching. If *you* don't understand the "why," you cannot establish a context for learning that will be both meaningful and believable for your students. So, for example, think through why it is important for your students to understand the parts of a sentence and why it is important that they know how to convert fractions into decimals before you teach these topics. Push yourself beyond simply arguing that "it's on the test," and reflect on why knowing these things matters.

Identify powerful questions and pursuits that are worthy of accomplishment. Research problems, challenges, and projects in your school and local community, and think about how students might participate or contribute. Could your developing English language learners read to younger students? Could your math students collect data for a research study? Could your science students remove invasive plant species from the schoolyard or neighborhood park? Could your social studies students advocate for a policy in front of town officials? Finding projects or activities with external significance allows students to experience the broader context for what they are learning. They see how the skills and knowledge they are developing can be used in the world.

Co-create projects/summative assignments with students. Even the best projects a teacher comes up with may leave some students feeling marginalized. Once the project parameters are established, collaborate with your students to determine various ways its tasks could be accomplished. Ask the students to develop the directions or actions with you. Not only will this give them an increased stake in their project roles and responsibilities, it will also leave them better prepared to troubleshoot failures or dead ends and find alternate approaches. When students are invited to co-create summative assignments, they are much more invested in their performance and in their learning (Fullan & Langworthy, 2014; Zmuda, Ullman, & Curtis, 2015).

Create a standing opportunity to "pursue interesting." We've already discussed the goal-clarifying advantage of providing a scoring guide or rubric when students are working on complicated projects and products. These tools provide a second way to support meaningful learning. Try inviting any student who wants to undertake a project that is more personalized or internally significant to propose an alternative approach, and ask them to use the scoring guide or rubric to justify this alternative approach as an appropriate way to measure the established learning goals.

Whenever possible, connect assignments to authentic audiences. As you consider the work you want your students to do, think of who the audience for it might be, how your students might bring the work to that audience, and how the audience might provide feedback (Zmuda, Ullman, & Curtis, 2015). For example, a high school social studies teacher and her students reviewed a new juvenile justice law in Colorado and petitioned state legislators to revise it. A group of 1st graders created an interactive audio map for visitors to the school, incorporating nonstandard units of measure and reference points a person might use to navigate from the main office to classrooms and other spaces (e.g., the nurse's office, the library). In Devon, England, a class of 8-year-olds published their original findings on how bumblebees can be trained to forage from certain flowers in a prestigious scientific journal (http://rsbl.royalsocietypublishing.

org/content/7/2/168). Many websites, online tools, and virtual competitions, such as LitGenius, MuseumBox, and the annual Google Science Fair, are set up to allow students to create and share ideas as well as evaluate others' work. Providing students with an authentic audience establishes a community context for their learning that provides immediate and useful feedback.

Encourage students to set their own goals. The prescribed goals for an assignment are non-negotiable, but allowing students to set additional goals of their own can increase their personal investment in the work. Try giving your students a framework like SMART (goals that are Specific, Measurable, Achievable, Results-focused, and Time-bound) to help them articulate their goals, and then help them track their progress toward these goals over time. Encouraging personal goal setting shows students respect, and it allows them to establish a personal context in every assignment and learning experience.

Challenge

The question associated with the engagement key of **challenge** is **"How does it stretch my students?"**

Getting students fully engaged in their learning requires that they feel appropriately challenged by the work. The work is not too hard or too easy. It represents a struggle, but a "reasonable amount" of struggle that students feel equipped to overcome.

Because challenge is based on students' current abilities, it is very much a relative term; what may be challenging for one student may not be challenging for another. Thus, when you think about challenge, you have to consider students' perceptions—both of the work itself and of their own abilities to master the work—to determine what represents a reasonable struggle (Zimmerman, 2000). Challenge also requires you to consider not just the design of the assignment but also where and how often you might need to provide feedback that will support your students when they struggle. Research shows that if students receive regular corrective and descriptive feedback in relation to their current challenge, they are more likely to see it as something that helps them achieve their goal rather than as judgment or indication of failure (Hattie & Timperley, 2007). Regular feedback also allows them to experience how focused, corrective effort and progress go hand in hand.

Why Challenge Matters to Students

Students' sense of how challenging the work they are being asked to do is directly affects their ability to engage in the work. When they face a new assignment or learning task, they generally ask themselves two questions: (1) "Is this work worthy of my effort and attention—not too hard and not too easy?" and (2) "Am I up to the challenge?"

There's a lot going on behind these questions. If students see the work as beneath their current abilities ("boring," "a waste of time"), there is no incentive to engage. If they perceive the work as something that should be "easy" but won't be easy for them, given their current skills and abilities, they can be reluctant to try. When this pattern repeats over time, students who have fallen behind also fall into apathy ("I'm too stupid for all of this"). If students size up the work as difficult and probably outside of their current abilities, they can easily become frustrated and give up ("I *knew* this would be impossible!"). But if students see the assignment as demanding but also feel that they are up to the challenge, they're positioned to be fully engaged in their learning ("Yeah, this is complicated and tough, but I'm ready. Bring it!").

What You Can Do to Provide Challenge

You've no doubt been told that the goal is to teach within students' zone of proximal development (Vygotsky, 1978), that "sweet spot" where students are learning at the outer edge of their abilities. But finding that perfect level of challenge can be tricky, especially because each student has a different sweet spot. Here are a few suggestions for finding and managing the right level of challenge in your lessons.

Build flexible assignments to challenge students where they are. Because challenge is relative to each student, you will need to design learning tasks that are flexible enough to challenge a range of student abilities. In general, assignments that provide students with choice tend to provide the most flexibility in terms of challenge.

First, get good information about your students' current abilities to ensure that you are providing assignments to grow their performance. That means looking closely at their achievement data and classwork to figure out what they can do and considering what the next step in their development should be.

You also want to be sure students have different access points into the assignment by providing options around the 5 T's—Time, Task, Team, Technique, and Territory:

1. *Time:* Establish flexible due dates, or let students chose how quickly or slowly they will work through a particular assignment.

2. *Task:* Permit students to adjust the learning task to reflect their interests and learning needs.

3. *Team:* Allow students choices about whether they will work alone or with others and who the members of their team will be.

4. *Technique:* Provide options related to how students might carry out an assignment, and allow them to choose which strategies make the most sense to them and what process they feel will best help them learn.

5. *Territory:* Give students some autonomy about where they will work, how they will manage their materials, and the kind of work environment they would like (e.g., quiet or noisy, seated or moving around).

Identify and address the underlying skills embedded in assignments. Sometimes it's the "soft skills" you take for granted that present a barrier to student success and engagement. Examples might be the ability to identify credible sources when writing a research paper; the communication skills necessary to share ideas, express concerns, or ask for assistance when working in groups; and the ability to use spreadsheet software to collect, analyze, and present project data. To help yourself more accurately judge an assignment's level of challenge so that you can properly support students' efforts to meet that challenge, try the following:

- Identify and articulate the underlying skills right up front, both when you're designing the task and when you're explaining the task to students.

- Prepare quick tutorials for students who need assistance but don't want to sit down with you or prefer to access this help discreetly or independently. These tutorials can take many forms—a prepared collection of helpful hints, a short video, "Top 10" tips for working smarter not harder, and so on.

- Provide opportunities for students to work with you individually or in small groups on a particular underlying skill. Frame the work by using a hook question or statement, and identify a window of time. For example: *So you keep getting feedback on your paper about "showing not telling." Want to learn three strategies to help you do that? Come join me for a 15-minute work session.* This approach honors students' areas of struggle but also feels practical and efficient. The shortness of the session means they can quickly return to the challenge at hand.

Manage students' perceptions of the work. Many times it's not that the work is too hard for students, it's that the students *think* the work is too hard. Those who believe that they won't be able to complete a task correctly or well are less likely engage in it fully, and some will not attempt it at all (Dweck, 2006). There is a process you can follow to help your students view challenging work in a new and positive way.

First, focus on breaking down the work into smaller chunks (Willis, 2011). Often it's the length of the assignment or the volume of work that students find intimidating, not the work itself. So instead of asking students to write a 10-page paper, have them write five 2-page papers and then connect these papers together for the final draft. Instead of assigning one long story for them to read on their own, break the story down into multiple episodes and ask them to read one part and stop to discuss it before moving on to the next part.

Second, remind students of what they've accomplished already, and how these accomplishments have prepared them for the new challenges ahead. For example, show them how the work they did successfully last week (multiplying 1-digit numbers) is similar to the work they're about to undertake (multiplying 2-digit numbers). Point out how their demonstrated success analyzing short Shakespearean sonnets has given them the tools they need to understand and enjoy *Romeo and Juliet.* And don't forget to call attention to the logic of your instructional design, which we discussed in our conversation about clarity (see p. 17). Show students where their learning currently stands within your coordinated and thoughtful plan for the course, the year, or the subject area.

Third, before you launch students on an assignment that you think they'll perceive as being too difficult, lead a whole-class activity to identify the skills or background knowledge necessary to complete the assignment successfully. Then provide a quick review of these skills and knowledge, either right then with the whole group or via small-group instruction with students who need it. In a similar vein, periodically set aside time for opt-in "skill lessons." You might review effective study techniques in the week leading up to a big test, for example, or address organizational structures and strategies for meeting deadlines while students are working on a huge research project.

Build students' self-confidence. If you want students to tackle new challenges in a way that is fully engaged, you have to help them see that they are capable and believe they are up to the challenge the assignment presents. We can suggest two powerful ways to do this.

The first is to help students accurately self-monitor and self-evaluate. Many either overestimate or grossly underestimate their capacity to manage the tasks before them. Show them how to develop a realistic self-assessment of their readiness for the tasks they face. For instance, you might have students rate themselves on a list of skills required for an upcoming assignment but with this twist: they must provide evidence from their past work in order to justify each rating. Or you might have students keep a portfolio of their work and, from time to time, ask them to write a reflection about what they know, how they've grown, and what they still need to know. It's critical that you talk with them about how they will leverage their current abilities (or compensate for areas where they may not be as strong) throughout the task. For instance, a student who can pinpoint that not knowing his multiplication tables is the reason for his low math scores can take corrective action and make immediate improvements. You can guide more accurate self-assessment by always giving "growth-oriented feedback." Yes, pointing out errors is part of a teacher's job, but you want to accompany this with suggestions for how the student can improve.

A second way to help students see themselves as capable is to give them plenty of chances to *be* capable. Foster self-reliance. Rather than giving students the answer, show them how to find the answer for themselves.

Gradually release responsibility. Many students will feel at first that they cannot handle challenging work on their own. They will want to rely on you. You can build their confidence and ability through a series of intentional, diminishing supports. Start by clearly communicating that by the end of the lesson (or unit or assignment), you expect everyone in the class to be working independently. Then carefully script your instruction and support so that you set up students to meet that expectation by waiting longer after you check in with students before providing feedback, reducing the amount of support you provide at each check in, gradually decreasing the amount of feedback you provide, and urging students to rely more on their growing self-assessment abilities. Have students create records that indicate the amount of focused practice/effort they are investing and the resulting progress. They can use a visual graph or collect scored assignments over time on a particular area of focus (e.g., writing an effective thesis statement, ability to analyze data). To draw even more self-reflective attention to students' expanding abilities and how much progress they've made, ask them to create "progress snapshots"—statements that indicate what they focused on, how long it took, and how they might apply this learning to meet future challenges.

Culture

The question associated with the engagement key of **culture** is **"How do I show my support?"**

All good teachers work hard to know their students in order to provide encouragement, assistance, and a more customized learning experience. However, these positive teacher–student relationships do not guarantee a positive and supportive classroom culture. To achieve that, teachers need to do more than just get along with students. They need to partner with students to jointly create a safe and respectful environment where deep thinking is expected, messy, and out in the open (Berger, 2003; Fullan & Langworthy, 2014).

Let's break this definition down a bit. *Expected* indicates that every student is involved in deep thinking—there are no bystanders to the heavy lifting that meaning making requires. *Messy* means that because students are working on rich problems, texts, or tasks, everyone knows that there will be dead ends, mistakes, and failures that need revision. *Out in the open* signifies that the deep thinking will be conducted as a dialogue *with* students and *among* students. It means everyone will be testing out assumptions, perspectives, or solutions; finding and examining evidence; and engaging in further inquiry.

Clearly, this kind of classroom culture goes way beyond student surveys and demonstrations of caring (although those are still very important). To achieve it, there are some prerequisites.

First, it's imperative to incorporate challenging assignments that push all students to experiment and problem solve. As a teacher, your role is to even the playing field so that every student can struggle productively (Howard, 2011; Tough, 2013). You want everyone thinking deeply, developing and testing out solution paths, articulating their reasoning, and becoming more comfortable with ambiguity. In life, the "right" answer is not always readily apparent, and there may not be a linear path to finding it.

Second, you have to be mindful of your own and your students' *currencies,* which are the skills, abilities, knowledge, and interests that people acquire in life, recognize as valuable, and "invest" or "spend" in order to get what they want (Jackson, 2011). Part of your job is to help your students acquire new forms of currency—a broad range of academic, social, technical, and organizational knowledge and skills—so that they will be well-prepared to thrive in all sorts of environments and cultural contexts. And part of developing learning partnerships is being open to what motivates your students. In other words, to build a connected, interdependent classroom, you must look for ways to value the social, emotional, interest-based, and skill-based currencies your students bring to the table even as you show them how they might use the new and different currencies you value to acquire new forms of capital. In doing so, you honor your students' ways of knowing, understanding, and representing information.

Why a Supportive Culture Matters to Students

Students "size up" the teacher and their peers within the first few days of school, seeking answers to questions like "Do they believe I can do great things, and will they hold me accountable?" "Is this classroom a space where I can dig deeper into challenges?" "Do I feel safe and respected here?" and "What happens if I fail?"

These are high-stakes questions. If students do not feel that they have a safety net of support and a common understanding of what they can expect from their teacher and their peers, they are less likely to connect deeply to the content and conversations that go on in the classroom (Berger, 2003).

What You Can Do to Establish a Supportive Classroom Culture

Provide work that is on grade level. Students need differentiated assignments that are both challenging and feasible. Assignments that are above grade level and out of reach can trigger frustration and despair. But assignments that are below grade level can also lead to frustration—along with hopelessness and even resentment—because they send the message that students are not up to the challenge of the grade-level expectations. So start with work that is clearly on grade level and then consider what can be adjusted to make it appropriately challenging. Can you eliminate some of the problems? Can you provide background knowledge that gets students interested in the topic? Can you use various texts to provide access to key information? Ultimately, the goal is to create a classroom culture of high expectations that will engage students in meeting or exceeding grade-level challenges. You convey these expectations by giving students work that is worthy of them.

Set the expectation that learning is not efficient or linear—it's messy. Learning happens through an ongoing cycle of action-feedback-reflection: "What can I do? How did it work? What can I do next?" One way to set this expectation is to build regular opportunities for revision into the learning process. Unfortunately, the messiness of learning may not line up with your pacing guide. Here are two strategies that honor both the inherent messiness of deep learning and the reality of time limitations.

First, have students work in teams to examine exit tickets or other forms of formative assessment to identify common mistakes and misunderstandings. Each team should develop a "findings report" for the rest of class that might include skill reminders, helpful hints, or a set of examples and non-examples.

Second, regularly use rubrics or scoring tools to evaluate the current quality of student performance, and always return feedback that includes one or two concrete, actionable steps that students can take to improve or course-correct. If you want students to see their development as cumulative rather than summative, you can't wait for the results of the final assignment; you must provide feedback along the way.

Build a culture of critique. If the task is designed to promote student ownership, all students need time to revisit and revise their work, guided by feedback from you, their peers, and even experts from the community or in the field, through virtual means if necessary. Feedback can be complimentary, but it should also be constructively critical. It should focus on improvement: good ideas that students might develop further and suggestions that can lead them to pursue a deeper understanding of the problem, revise the model, articulate a statement more clearly, and so on. When students come to expect criticism that is respectful and useful, they take their work more seriously. They're more likely to invest themselves in revision and improvement—not solely for a better grade but because they really care about the quality of their work.

Establish an understanding of your learning partnership. Work with students to create a classroom contract that delineates what the teacher and the students can expect from one another. (Ideally, this is something you'd do in the first few days of school, but it's never too late to get started.) Here is an example of a classroom contract appropriate for students in grades 6–12, developed by a New York City public school (Zmuda, Ullman, & Curtis, 2015):

- I have a right to learn in a safe environment.
- I have a right to be treated with respect.
- I have a right to understand the purpose of an assignment.
- I have a right to clear expectations about what is expected from me.
- I have a right to get assistance in a timely manner when I have a question or problem.
- I have a right to get feedback on my work so I can improve it.
- I have a right to make mistakes and learn from them.
- I have a right to advocate for myself and others. (p. 55)

You can use this classroom contract as a rough draft (ask your students revise it to make it their own), or you can present it as a model (e.g., the number statements to aim for, how to phrase statements) as you and your students create your own contract. Whatever classroom contract you and your students generate, be sure to revisit it periodically throughout the year, adding to it or revising it as needed. This classroom contract can also serve as a self-evaluation tool and as a tool for evaluating group and classroom culture.

Don't "save" students from struggle. Struggle can be productive when it's guided by probing questions that help students unearth what they think, what evidence their conclusions are based on, and what alternate interpretations or approaches might be possible (Zmuda, 2010). Here is a set of probing questions for your consideration:

- What do you mean by _____?
- Can you elaborate? Tell me more.
- What are you assuming when you say that?
- How do the data support your conclusion?
- How does that square with what _____ (e.g., the text, a peer) says?
- Is it really either/or? Might there be different "right" answers or ways of thinking about this?

Modeling these questions consistently helps students find value in the struggle. It helps them move away from trying to get the "right" answer on the first try and pushes them to think more deeply and engage more fully in authentic learning.

Provide a safety net of support. Fully engaged learning requires risk. Attend to and openly address your students' fears about failing, pointing out that learning means pushing into new territories, following interesting paths, and doubling back and trying again when the trail doesn't take you where you wanted to go. One way to help students understand that failure isn't fatal or final is to create a safety net of support that will catch them whenever they happen to fall. Here are some suggestions for how you might do that:

- Make yourself available, physically and virtually, for student questions and concerns about an assignment.
- Encourage students to create a running record of their process or approach on a given assignment so that you will have insight into their methods and they will be able to refer back to their own problem-solving solutions.
- Set up consistent opportunities for all students to conference with you one on one to unearth challenges and co-create actions.
- Provide feedback on student work submitted as a Google Doc or MS Word document through the software's comment feature.
- Set up study groups as a way of helping students learn from one another.
- Establish and share a support plan that spells out how you will step in to help students before they get in real trouble. That way, students can focus on learning rather than on trying not to fail.
- Bring in volunteer tutors and mentors to provide additional support.
- Conduct regular review or reteaching sessions so that students know that they have multiple opportunities to "get it."
- Create a classroom resource center where students can find additional guidance and materials that will help them when they get stuck.
- Teach students strategies for getting unstuck in various scenarios (e.g., when completing homework, when taking a standardized test).

Real Engagement:
Why It's Worth It

When you walk into a classroom and feel that productive buzz of every student working intently and being personally invested in his or her own learning, it can seem almost magical. But, as we've argued in this book, real engagement isn't magic. Real engagement is real, and it's within your grasp if you consistently invest in and attend to its four keys: **clarity**, **context**, **challenge**, and **culture**.

It will take some work on your part—there's no getting around it. You will have to rethink some of your assignments. You will have to open yourself to being a real partner with your students. You will encounter some challenges and meet a few setbacks. You will still get frustrated when a carefully planned lesson doesn't take off as you hoped. Planning for real engagement takes the same willingness to try, to fail, to revise, and to try again that you want to instill in your students. If you want your students to take risks, to go beyond the parameters of an assignment, and to personally invest in their learning, you have to go first.

But it's worth the investment, and here's why. Real engagement resurrects *interesting*. It resurrects *passion*. It resurrects *joy*. Real engagement creates an environment of mutual respect, where your students value the time and effort you put into teaching them, and you value the energy and the risk they invest in their own learning. Real engagement empowers your students to go beyond the classroom, beyond the lesson, and beyond the curriculum to solve their own problems and, ultimately, to build their own future.

Yes, real engagement can garner you high scores on your teacher evaluation and the satisfaction that comes from helping your students learn in meaningful ways, but it changes you, too. It gives your teaching a jolt of purpose. You will stop seeing planning as a matter of compliance—of jumping through the standards hoops and keeping up with the pacing guide. With real engagement, planning becomes a design experience of considering and overcoming real challenges to student learning. You will stop seeing teaching as the process of dragging students through the curriculum. With real engagement, teaching becomes a newly powerful and living thing, a creative collaboration between you and your students. And you will stop seeing grading as a soul-sucking mountain of paperwork. With real engagement, grading becomes a way to continue the conversation you start in the classroom and push students to reach even higher. In the end, real engagement doesn't just get your students more involved; it re-engages you and helps you make the kind of difference that you became a teacher to make.

To give your feedback on this publication and
be entered into a drawing for a free ASCD
Arias e-book, please visit
www.ascd.org/ariasfeedback

ASCD | arias™

ENCORE

THE NEXT STEPS

Here's how to use the four keys to engagement to help yourself and your colleagues move toward real engagement schoolwide.

Next Steps for Teachers

If you're a teacher and you're ready to start applying each of the four keys to engagement in your classroom, here are a few more steps you can take:

☐ **Clarity.** Take time to fully unpack and understand your standards. If you're not completely sure what you are doing, it is hard for you to design thoughtful and meaningful lessons for students.

☐ **Context.** Find your own personal "why" for everything that you teach. Start every lesson design experience by first asking yourself, "Why am I teaching this? Why is this important? Why does this topic or skill matter to me? Why does student engagement in this topic or skill matter to me?" Understanding your personal "why" will keep you focused in the face of any challenges you may encounter.

☐ **Challenge.** Push yourself to work within but at the outer edges of your own teaching ability. Select at least one strategy from this book that presents a stretch for you—and jump in.

☐ **Culture.** Don't try to go it alone. Align your efforts with others in your building, or join an online community of teachers who are attempting to put these strategies into practice.

We also invite you to evaluate your own current level of engagement using the interactive tool at www.mindstepsinc.com/engagement. You can begin to address the four keys to real engagement in the order recommended by your results.

Next Steps for Teacher-Leaders or Instructional Coaches

☐ **Clarity.** Focus on helping teachers understand what real engagement is and the difference between real engagement and mere compliance. Then help them assess the current level of real engagement in their classroom. This will position them to understand where they need to start with their engagement efforts.

☐ **Context.** Prompt teachers to identify personal reasons for real engagement. Help them to think through the benefits it will bring (e.g., "My students will stop getting into petty fights and focus on the lesson," or "My students will start to care more about their work"). By getting teachers to articulate the value of real engagement in personal terms, you are helping them buy into the work that securing it will require. Also be sure to underline the connection between any strategy that you give them and their personal goals or classroom situation. When teachers see the value of your suggestions, they are more likely to take action.

☐ **Challenge.** Build an arsenal of resources teachers can use to secure real engagement, including model lessons and strategies. Do your homework by making sure you understand the various challenges presented by each of these strategies. Guide teachers toward those strategies that push them but are still within the boundaries of what they are able to implement now.

☐ **Culture.** Offer structured support around the four keys to real engagement. Create a safety net for teachers that anticipates where they may struggle as they implement the strategies you have given them. With prior preparation, you'll be able to deliver just-in-time support that will keep teachers going.

Next Steps for Administrators

☐ **Clarity.** Conduct walkthroughs with key staff to determine whether students are really engaged or merely compliant, and develop a plan for helping teachers foster real engagement in every lesson, every day. Share examples of engaged behavior and compliant behavior with staff to help them develop a more concrete understanding of what you are looking for and to establish a clear and common vocabulary around engagement. During evaluations, make sure your feedback to teachers includes clear and concrete examples of engaged and compliant behavior that you observed during their lessons. The better you're able to articulate what real engagement is and how to recognize it, the better you position your staff to visualize and then meet your goals for schoolwide engagement.

☐ **Context.** Engage your staff in a conversation around real engagement. Focus on why real engagement is so important in the context of whole-school goals: the work you are trying to accomplish with your students at your school.

☐ **Challenge.** Provide teachers with growth-oriented feedback to help them recognize and take steps toward real engagement in their classroom. Also seek out differentiated professional development opportunities that further teachers' individual abilities to provide real engagement.

☐ **Culture.** Offer teachers multiple opportunities to learn strategies for real engagement, and ensure that they have time to try a strategy, receive nonevaluative feedback, and revise their approach before they are evaluated on the level of student engagement in their classroom. You want teachers to feel safe enough to take strategic risks and make changes that will be substantial and meaningful.

References

Barron, B., & Darling-Hammond, L. (2007). Teaching for meaningful learning: A review of research on inquiry-based and cooperative learning. *Edutopia.* Retrieved from http://www.edutopia.org/pdfs/edutopia-teaching-for-meaningful-learning.pdf

Berger, R. (2003). *An ethic of excellence: Building a culture of craftsmanship with students.* Portsmouth, NH: Heinemann.

Dweck, C. (2006). *Mindset: The new psychology of success.* New York: Random House.

Fullan, M., & Langworthy, M. (2014, January). *A rich seam: How new pedagogies find deep learning.* London: Pearson. Available: http://www.michaelfullan.ca/wp-content/uploads/2014/01/3897.Rich_Seam_web.pdf

Hattie, J., & Timperley, H. (2007). The power of feedback. *Review of Educational Research, 77*(1), 81–112.

Holm, M. (2011). Project-based instruction: A review of the literature on effectiveness in prekindergarten through 12th grade classrooms. *Rivier Academic Journal, 7*(2), 1–13. Available: http://bie.org/object/document/project_based_learning_a_review_of_the_literature_on_effectiveness

Howard, J. (2011, September 21). Feedback is fundamental [Blog post]. *The Efficiency Institute.* Retrieved from http://www.efficacy.org/Resources/TheEIPointofView/tabid/233/ctl/ArticleView/mid/678/articleId/426/Feedback-is-Fundamental.aspx

Jackson, R. R. (2011). *How to motivate reluctant learners.* Alexandria, VA: ASCD.

Tough, P. (2013). *How children succeed: Grit, curiosity, and the hidden power of character.* New York: Mariner Books.

Vygotsky, L. S. (1978). *Mind in society: The development of higher psychological processes.* Cambridge, MA: Harvard University Press.

Wiggins, G., & McTighe, J. (2005). *Understanding by Design.* Alexandria, VA: ASCD.

Wiggins, G., & McTighe, J. (2011). *The Understanding by Design guide to creating high-quality units.* Alexandria, VA: ASCD.

Willis, J. (2011, April 14). A neurologist makes the case for the video game model as a learning tool [Blog post]. *Edutopia.* Retrieved from http://www.edutopia.org/blog/neurologist-makes-case-video-game-model-learning-tool

Zimmerman, B. (2000). Self-efficacy: An essential motive to learn. *Contemporary Educational Psychology, 25,* 82–91. Available: http://www.itari.in/categories/ability_to_learn/self_efficacy_an_essential_motive_to_learn.pdf

Zmuda, A. (2010). *Breaking free from myths about teaching and learning: Innovation as an engine for student success.* Alexandria, VA: ASCD.

Zmuda, A., Ullman, D., & Curtis, G. (2015). *Learning personalized: The evolution of the contemporary classroom.* San Francisco: Jossey-Bass.

Related Resources

At the time of publication, the following ASCD resources were available (ASCD stock numbers appear in parentheses). For up-to-date information about ASCD resources, go to www.ascd.org. You can search the complete archives of *Educational Leadership* at http://www.ascd.org/el.

ASCD EDge©
Exchange ideas and connect with other educators interested in various topics, including inspiring student motivation, on the social networking site ASCD EDge at http://edge.ascd.org.

Print Products
Encouragement in the Classroom: How Do I Help Students Stay Positive and Focused? (ASCD Arias) by Joan Young (#114049)

How to Motivate Reluctant Learners (Mastering the Principles of Great Teaching series) by Robyn R. Jackson (#100076)

The Motivated Student: Unlocking the Enthusiasm for Learning by Bob Sullo (#109028)

Role Reversal: Achieving Uncommonly Excellent Results in the Student-Centered Classroom by Mark Barnes (#113004)

ASCD PD Online© Courses
Understanding Student Motivation, 2nd edition (#PD11OC106)
This and other online courses are available at www.ascd.org/pdonline.

DVDs
A Visit to a Motivated Classroom (#603384)
Engaging Students with Poverty in Mind DVD series (#613041)

For more information: send e-mail to member@ascd.org; call 1-800-933-2723 or 703-578-9600, press 2; send a fax to 703-575-5400; or write to Information Services, ASCD, 1703 N. Beauregard St., Alexandria, VA 22311-1714 USA.

About the Authors

Allison Zmuda is a full-time education consultant focused on curriculum, assessment, and instruction who works with educators to make learning for students challenging, possible, and worthy of the attempt. A former high school teacher, she is the author of seven books, including *The Competent Classroom* (2001), *Transforming Schools* (2004), *Breaking Free from Myths About Teaching and Learning* (2010), and, most recently, *Learning Personalized: The Evolution of a Contemporary Classroom* (2015). In addition, Zmuda launched and curates the online community Learning Personalized (http://learningpersonalized.com) to share the ideas, innovations, and accomplishments of students, parents, and educators. You can follow her on Twitter at @allison_zmuda or reach her via e-mail at allison@ allisonzmuda.com.

Robyn R. Jackson, PhD, is a former high school teacher and middle school administrator. She is the founder and president of Mindsteps Inc., a professional development firm for teachers and administrators that provides workshops and materials designed to help any teacher reach every student. Jackson is the author of *The Instructional Leader's Guide to Strategic Conversations with Teachers* (2008), *Never Work Harder Than Your Students and Other Principles of Great Teaching* (2009), the REVERE Award-winning *Never Underestimate Your Teachers: Instructional Leadership for Excellence in Every Classroom* (2013), and *You Can Do This: Hope and Help for New Teachers* (2014), as well as the how-to guides in the Mastering the Principles of Great Teaching series. You can sign up for Jackson's monthly e-newsletter at www.mindstepsinc.com, follow her on Twitter at @robyn_mindsteps, or reach her via e-mail at robyn@mindstepsinc.com.

WHAT KEEPS YOU UP AT NIGHT?

ASCD Arias begin with a burning question and then provide the answers you need today—in a convenient format you can read in one sitting and immediately put into practice. Available in both print and digital editions.

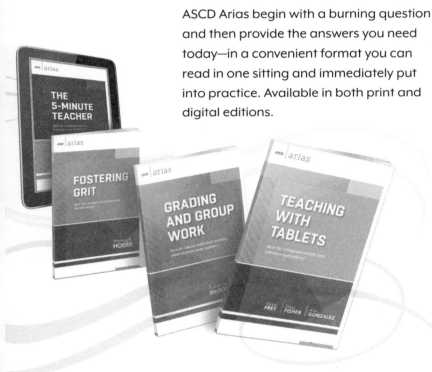

arias

THE 5-MINUTE TEACHER

arias

FOSTERING GRIT

Thomas R. HOERR

arias

GRADING AND GROUP WORK

Susan M. BROOK

arias

TEACHING WITH TABLETS

Nancy FREY | Douglas FISHER | Alex GONZALEZ

Answers You Need
from Voices You Trust

ASCD | arias™

For more information, go to www.ascdarias.org or call (toll-free in the United States and Canada) 800-933-ASCD (2723).

www.ascdarias.org